For Anna and Jarrett, with love.

Many thanks to Rob and Charlie.

Printed in China

Library of Congress Catalog Card Number: 2001119168

ISBN 1-887137-34-3

First U.S. edition, 2002

Photography - Ralph Homan, New Albany, IN and Margaret Viles, Beaufort, SC

Design - Elizabeth B. Swearingen-Edens

www.tisfortwins.com

T

is for
Twins

an ABC book by Mary Bond

Half Full Press Oakland, California

A

is for apples of my eyes.

Aa

B

is for babies, full of surprise.

C

is the cuddles
four arms can share.

D

is for the delight in a pair.

E is for energy. . .two busy bees.

Ee

F
is for fun. . .
doing as you please.

Ff

G

is for goodness.
You're sweet and kind.

H

is the happiness, together you find.

Hh

I

is the intrigue
you find in a toy.

J

is for two little
bundles of joy.

K is for kinship - together forever.

L

is for laughter
filling every endeavor.

M

is for multiples, strength in numbers.

N

is for napping - peaceful, restful slumbers.

O

is for any opportunity to
jump, jump, jump.

P is for pumpkin, sweet pea, and sugarlump.

Q

is for quiet times, secrets shared.

R

is for running,
running everywhere.

S

is for the special things you two do.

Ss

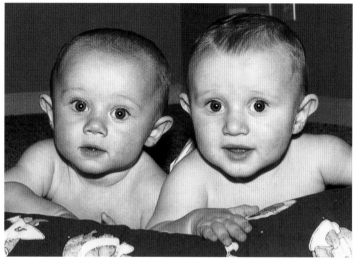

Tt

T

is for twins, of course, to you.

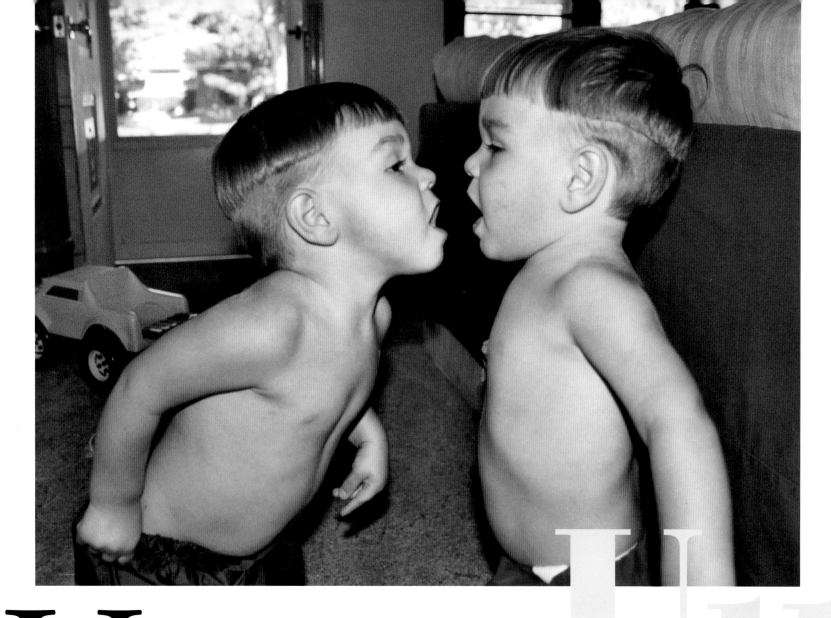

U is understanding your unique bond.

V

is your vitality, of which we're so fond.

W

is the wonder you
discover every day.

Ww

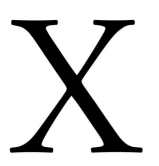

X

is the excitement you find in your play.

Y is for yesterday's memories, anticipating what's in store.

Z is for your remarkable zest. We couldn't love you more.